Balinese Cats

Stephanie Finne

Checkerboard
Library

An Imprint of Abdo Publishing
www.abdopublishing.com

www.abdopublishing.com

Published by Abdo Publishing, a division of ABDO, PO Box 398166, Minneapolis, MN 55439.
Copyright © 2015 by Abdo Consulting Group, Inc. International copyrights reserved in all
countries. No part of this book may be reproduced in any form without written permission from
the publisher. Checkerboard Library™ is a trademark and logo of Abdo Publishing.

Printed in the United States of America, North Mankato, Minnesota.
032014
092014

Cover Photo: Photo by Helmi Flick
Interior Photos: Alamy p. 1; Getty Images p. 17; Glow Images pp. 5, 15; Photos by Helmi Flick
    pp. 7, 9, 13; Minden Pictures pp. 11, 19, 20–21; Thinkstock p. 13

Series Coordinator: Bridget O'Brien
Editors: Rochelle Baltzer, Tamara L. Britton, Megan M. Gunderson
Art Direction: Renée LaViolette

Library of Congress Cataloging-in-Publication Data

Finne, Stephanie, author.
  Balinese cats / Stephanie Finne.
    pages cm. -- (Cats)
  Audience: Ages 8-12.
  Includes index.
  ISBN 978-1-62403-322-3
  1. Balinese cat--Juvenile literature. I. Title.
  SF449.B34F56 2015
  636.8'3--dc23
                        2013046912

Contents

Lions, Tigers, and Cats

The cats adored by millions of pet owners are descendants of African wild cats. These cats were known for their hunting abilities.

Eventually, humans saw the benefit of taming cats. People valued their ability to hunt **rodents** and keep grain free from pests. So, cats were **domesticated** more than 3,500 years ago.

Throughout time, humans have **bred** cats to have the qualities they desired. Today, there are more than 40 different cat breeds. They share the family **Felidae** with 36 other species. That means lovable companions like the domestic cat are related to lions and cougars!

Some **domestic** cats still look like their wild cousins. Others are beautiful animals ready to be in cat shows. Many, like the Balinese, are prized for their intelligence and affectionate nature.

The Balinese cat

Balinese Cats

Balinese cats are Siamese cats with long-haired coats. In 1928, a long-haired Siamese was registered with the **Cat Fanciers' Federation**. But it wasn't until the 1950s that people began **breeding** long-haired Siamese kittens.

In the 1950s, cats owned by Siamese breeders Marion Dorsey and Helen Smith had long-haired kittens. Dorsey and Smith decided to breed more of these beautiful cats. In 1955, the first long-haired Siamese was entered in a cat show.

People loved the new look. However, breeders wanted the long-haired Siamese to have a different name. The cat's grace reminded Smith of Balinese dancers. So, she suggested the name *Balinese*. The name was accepted.

In 1979, the **Cat Fanciers' Association** recognized Balinese with seal, blue, chocolate, and lilac **pointed** coats. These are traditional Siamese colors. Cats with lynx point, **tortie** point, or red and cream point coats were called Javanese. In 2008, **breeders** voted to combine the two breeds as the Balinese.

Today, all colors of Balinese are accepted around the world.

Qualities

Balinese owners love this **breed**'s looks as well as its personality. Balinese cats are curious. They love to play. But, they demand a lot of attention. Balinese also get into a lot of mischief. Do not leave your Balinese cat alone for long periods of time!

Balinese cats make great family pets. They are very loving. This makes them good with children and other pets. These cats want to be involved in everything you do. They want to be your best friend!

Like Siamese cats, Balinese are talkative. Sometimes they even talk to themselves! But, their voices are softer than a Siamese cat's. If you want a **vocal**, affectionate, playful cat, the Balinese is the breed for you.

The Balinese cat's curiosity can lead to trouble. These intelligent cats can open drawers to find hidden objects!

Coat and Color

The Balinese cat is best known for its soft, silky, long-haired coat. On the body, the coat is one-half inch to two inches (1 to 5 cm) long. The fur on the long, **plumed** tail can be five inches (13 cm) long.

The Balinese's coat has only one layer. There is no undercoat. This makes the coat lie flat against the cat's body. It also helps keep the coat from **matting** and **shedding**. Because of this, the Balinese is easy to groom. A quick brush is all it needs, which many owners appreciate.

The Balinese's coat can be any color. The most common are the traditional Siamese colors of seal, chocolate, blue, and lilac **point** coats. Other Balinese colors include red, cream, and the **tabby** and **tortie** patterns. Balinese fans have a wide variety of options!

As it gets older, a Balinese's coat will become darker.

Size

Balinese are medium-sized, slender cats. Females often weigh five to seven pounds (2.5 to 3.2 kg). Males are slightly larger. They weigh six to eight pounds (2.7 to 3.6 kg).

The Balinese cat's triangular head features a tapered **muzzle** and a straight nose. The almond-shaped eyes are always blue. They are slanted toward the ears. The ears are large and pointed.

The Balinese is long and graceful. It is sleek with fine bones. But this skinny cat is very muscular! These strong, **agile** cats can leap from the floor to the top of the refrigerator in one graceful movement!

The Balinese cat's long legs end in oval paws.

Care

Cats are known as independent creatures, but your Balinese will depend on you for its care. Your cat will want to bury its waste. So, provide a **litter box** and make sure to clean it out every day. A scratching post will keep your cat from sharpening its claws on furniture and carpet. Your Balinese will also need toys to fetch and bat around.

Like all cats, your Balinese requires regular checkups with a veterinarian. Your pet will receive **vaccines** and an overall exam at its vet visit. The vet can also **spay** or **neuter** cats that will not be **bred**.

Finally, your Balinese needs your time! This breed is active and can be demanding. But, Balinese are also loving and friendly. Including your cat in everything you do will help make it happy and healthy.

Balinese kittens love to play!

Feeding

Caring for your cat includes providing a balanced diet. Choose a food that is labeled "complete and balanced." This food will contain everything your cat needs in a healthy diet.

There are three common ways to feed pet cats. Food can be measured out. This is called portion fed. It can be fed at specific times of day. This is called time fed. Or, food can always be available. This is called free fed.

There are different types of cat food, too. Dry foods help clean your cat's teeth. Semimoist foods are softer and do not need to be refrigerated. Canned foods are moist, but they spoil quickly. They must be refrigerated.

If needed, you can discuss types of food and feeding options with your vet. A vet can also suggest

cat treats. The right food in the right amount is important for helping your cat maintain a healthy weight. Along with food and treats, be sure to always provide fresh water for your cat.

Kittens need to eat more protein than adult Balinese.

Kittens

When they reach 7 to 12 months old, cats can reproduce. After mating, female cats are **pregnant** for about 65 days. When a cat gives birth, it is called kittening. Usually, four kittens are born in a single **litter**.

When the kittens are born, they are blind, deaf, and helpless. They can see and hear after 10 to 12 days. By this time, they also have teeth. When they are three weeks old, they begin to explore their surroundings.

For the first five weeks, kittens drink their mother's milk. Then, they begin to eat solid food. During these early weeks, their job is to learn and grow! When they are 12 to 16 weeks old, they are ready for a new loving home.

At birth, Balinese kittens have white coats. Their points develop color as they grow.

Buying a Kitten

Balinese cats are active and demand a lot of attention. They like to be involved in everything, even sharing their human's food! So, be sure you can give your Balinese a lot of your time.

If you decide to get a Balinese cat, find a reputable **breeder**. Good breeders sell healthy cats that have had **vaccinations**. Healthy cats will live for 10 to 15 years. Be sure you are ready for a long commitment!

Before bringing home your pet, be sure to get some supplies. Food and water dishes, food, and a **litter box** are the most important items to have on hand. You are now ready to enjoy time with your new friend!

The Balinese think of themselves as people. They make wonderful additions to any family.

Glossary

agile - able to move quickly or easily.

breed - a group of animals sharing the same ancestors and appearance. A breeder is a person who raises animals. Raising animals is often called breeding them.

Cat Fanciers' Association - a group that sets the standards for judging all breeds of cats.

Cat Fanciers' Federation - a regional cat registry that operates in the northeastern United States.

domestic - tame, especially relating to animals.

Felidae (FEHL-uh-dee) - the scientific Latin name for the cat family. Members of this family are called felids. They include lions, tigers, leopards, jaguars, cougars, wildcats, lynx, cheetahs, and domestic cats.

litter - all of the kittens born at one time to a mother cat.

litter box - a box filled with cat litter, which is similar to sand. Cats use litter boxes to bury their waste.

mat - to form into a tangled mass.

muzzle - an animal's nose and jaws.

neuter (NOO-tuhr) - to remove a male animal's reproductive glands.

plumed - relating to a large, showy feather or something that resembles one.

points - an animal's extremities, such as the feet, the ears, and the tail.

pregnant - having one or more babies growing within the body.

rodent - any of several related animals that have large front teeth for gnawing. Common rodents include mice, squirrels, and beavers.

shed - to cast off hair, feathers, skin, or other coverings or parts by a natural process.

spay - to remove a female animal's reproductive organs.

tabby - a coat pattern featuring stripes or splotches of a dark color on a lighter background. Individual hairs are banded with light and dark colors.

tortie (TAWR-tee) - another name for the tortoiseshell pattern, a coat featuring patches of black, orange, and cream.

vaccine (vak-SEEN) - a shot given to prevent illness or disease.

vocal - likely to express oneself with the voice.

Websites

To learn more about Cats,
visit **booklinks.abdopublishing.com**. These links are routinely monitored and updated to provide the most current information available.

Index